영웅 되기
Being a Superhero

리즈 쉬무일로프
그림 메리 비스워즈

www.kidkiddos.com
Copyright ©2019 by KidKiddos Books Ltd.
support@kidkiddos.com

All rights reserved. No part of this book may be reproduced in any form or by any electronic or mechanical means, including information storage and retrieval systems, without written permission from the publisher, except in the case of a reviewer, who may quote brief passages embodied in critical articles or in a review.
First edition

Translated from English by Tay Bake
영한 옮김 백태은
Korean editing by Yeji Park
교정 및 검수 박예지

Library and Archives Canada Cataloguing in Publication
Being a Superhero (Korean English Bilingual Edition)/ Liz Shmuilov
ISBN: 978-1-5259-4903-6 paperback
ISBN: 978-1-5259-4904-3 hardcover
ISBN: 978-1-5259-4902-9 eBook

Please note that the Korean and English versions of the story have been written to be as close as possible. However, in some cases they differ in order to accommodate nuances and fluidity of each language.

안녕 친구들! 내 이름은 마야야. 난 도마뱀이야. 내 단짝 친구 개구리 론이 영웅이 된 이야기를 들려주고 싶어.
Hi friends! My name is Maya. I am a lizard. I want to tell you a story about my best friend Ron the frog, who became a superhero.

어느 여름날, 난 론의 집에서 우리가 가장 좋아하는 영웅 이야기를 티비로 보고 있었어.
One summer day, I was at Ron's house watching our favorite superhero show.

"있잖아." 론이 갑자기 말했어. "영웅이 되는 건 정말 멋있는 것 같아. 그럼 다른 사람들을 도울 수 있잖아!"
"You know," Ron said suddenly, "it would be cool to be a superhero. Then we would be able to help others!"

"정말 좋은 생각이야!" 라고 대답하는데, 수많은 생각이 떠올랐어. "내가 코치가 돼서 영웅이 되는데 필요한 모든 것을 가르쳐 줄게!"
"That's a great idea!" I replied, millions of thoughts racing through my mind. "I could be your coach and teach you all the things a superhero needs to know!"

이 말을 들은 론의 얼굴엔 희망의 기운이 감돌았어.
As he heard this, a look of hope appeared on Ron's face.

"하지만 영웅은 초능력이 필요한걸." 론이 조용히 말했어.
"But every superhero needs a superpower," he said quietly.

난 잠시 생각했어. "네 초능력은 엄청나게 긴 점프야! 아, 그리고 끈적끈적한 손도!"
I thought for a moment. "Your superpower can be your talent in long jumps! Oh, and your sticky hands!"

"맞아!" 론이 기뻐 껑충 뛰었어.
"Yes!" Ron jumped with excitement.

"이제 옷을 만들자. 모두가 알아볼 수 있게." 내가 말했어.
"Now we need a costume. Something everyone will recognize," I said.

론은 방으로 달려가 빨간 티셔츠를 가져왔어. "여기다 큰 별을 그리자!"
Ron ran to his room and brought out a red shirt. "We can color a big star on this shirt!"

"좋은 생각이야!" 나는 미소지었어.
"망토는 어때?"
"Great idea!" I smiled.
"How about a cape?"

"내가 아끼는 담요를 사용하자!" 론이 외쳤어. 론의 눈은 반짝였지.
"We can use my favorite blanket!" exclaimed Ron. His eyes sparkled.

우린 곧바로 작업을 시작했고, 론의 티셔츠에 그림을 그려 넣었어.
We got straight to work, drawing and painting on Ron's shirt.

"너무 멋져! 진짜 영웅처럼 보일 거야!" 그림 그리기를 마친 뒤 내가 말했어.
"It looks amazing! You will look like a real superhero!" I said when we finished.

"오늘 내가 영웅이 되기 위한 중요한 몇 가지를 알려줄게. 바로 영웅의 세 가지 규칙이야."
"Today, I will teach you a few important things every superhero needs to know: The Three Superhero Rules."

벤치에 앉아서 나는 론에게 규칙을 설명하기 시작했어.
We sat down on the bench and I explained the rules to Ron.

"첫 번째 규칙. 그 어떤 어려운 상황이 닥쳐도 절대 포기하지 않는다."
"Rule number one: never give up, no matter how difficult the situation gets."

"두 번째 규칙. 다음에 더 잘할 수 있도록 실수로부터 배운다."
"Rule number two: learn from your mistakes, so that you can do better next time."

"세 번째 규칙. 어떤 일이든지 해낼 수 있다는 걸 절대 잊지 않는다!"
"Rule number three: always remember that you can do anything!"

우린 규칙들을 외우고 나서 나의 집으로 향했어.
We worked on memorizing the rules and then headed back to my house.

집에 오니까 내 동생 대니가 있었어. 대니는 속상해보였어.
When we got home, we met my little brother Danny. He looked upset.

"내가 가장 아끼는 장난감을 찾을 수가 없어!" 동생은 큰 소리로 울었어.
"I can't find my favorite toy!" he cried loudly.

난 론을 보고 속삭였어. "영웅을 위한 첫 번째 임무야!"
I glanced at Ron and whispered, "This seems like a mission for a Superhero!"

론은 웃으며 고개를 끄덕였어. "장난감이 어떻게 생겼니?" 론이 물었어.
Ron smiled and nodded. "What does the toy look like?" he asked.

"푹신푹신한 사자 인형이야. 티비 영웅 프로그램에서 나왔던." 대니가 얘기했어. "아주 크고 부드러워."
"It's my stuffed toy, the lion, from the superhero TV show," explained Danny. "It's big and soft."

"걱정 마. 우리가 찾아 줄게." 론은 동생을 안심시킨 뒤, 우리의 첫 번째 임무를 시작했어.
"Don't worry. We will find it," Ron assured him, and we began our first mission.

우린 모든 곳을 뒤졌어. 옷장 안, 찬장 옆, 식탁 뒤, 그리고 의자 아래까지. 장난감은 어디에도 보이지 않았어.
We looked everywhere—in closets, beside cupboards, behind tables and under chairs. The toy was nowhere to be found.

"너희는 뒷마당을 찾아봐. 난 여기서 계속 찾아볼게." 론이 말했어.
"You two should go look in the backyard, and I'll keep searching here," Ron suggested.

대니와 내가 밖에 막 나가려던 순간, 론의 목소리가 들렸어.
"찾았다! 내가 찾았어!"
Just as Danny and I stepped outside, we heard Ron's voice. "I found it! I found it!"

달려가 보니 론의 손에 조그마한 물건이 들려 있었어.
We ran to him and looked down at the small object in his hand.

"그건 내가 말한 사자 인형이 아니잖아." 대니가 찡그렸어. "내 인형은 크고 부드럽다구. 그런데 이건 작고 나무로 만들어졌잖아."
"That's not the lion I was talking about," Danny frowned. "My toy is big and soft, but this one is small and wooden."

론은 당황했지만, 재빨리 실망한 얼굴을 감추고 자신감을 내비쳤어.
Ron's face fell at first, but a look of determination quickly replaced the disappointment.

"걱정 마" 론이 말했어. "영웅의 첫 번째 규칙: 절대 포기하지 않는다!"
"No worries," he said. "Superhero rule number one: Never give up!"

"두 번째 규칙." 내가 덧붙였어. "실수로부터 배운다. 이제 크고, 부드럽고, 푹신푹신한 장난감을 찾아보자."
"Rule number two," I added, "Learn from your mistakes. We are looking for a BIG, SOFT, stuffed toy."

"부드럽고 큰 인형. 알았어!"" 론이 답했어.
"Soft and big. Got it!" Ron replied.

"그리고 세 번째 규칙" 내가 말했어. "어떤 일이든지 해낼 수 있는 사람이 누구더라?"
"And rule number three," I said. "Who can do anything?"

"난 영웅이고 어떤 일이든 해낼 수 있어!" 론이 신이 나서 외쳤어.
"I'm a Superhero and I can do anything!" yelled Ron enthusiastically.

"우린 영웅처럼 생각해야 해." 론이 말을 이어 갔어. "만약 장난감이 집 안에 없다면, 분명히 집 밖에 있을 거야. 그건 날지 못하니까 멀리 가진 못했을걸!"
"We have to think like superheroes," he continued. "If the toy is not in the house, it must be somewhere outside. It's not like it can fly away!"

론이 웃으며 하늘 위를 봤을 때, 론은 갑자기 굳고 말았어.
Ron giggled and looked up to the sky, but suddenly froze.

"뭘 쳐다보는 거야?" 궁금해진 난 위를 같이 쳐다봤어.
"What are you staring at?" I wondered, looking up also.

론이 큰 사과나무 위를 가리켰어.
Ron pointed to the top of our big apple tree.

"혹시 저거야…?" 나는 중얼거렸어.
"Is that…?" I began to mumble.

"내 장난감이야! 형이 찾았어!" 대니가 소리쳤어.
"My toy! You found it, Ron!" Danny exclaimed.

"그런데 어떻게 나무 위로 가서 저걸 가져오지?" 대니가 말했어.
"But how will we get it from the tree?" he added quietly.

"론이라면 쉽게 할 수 있지." 내가 말했어. "론은 초능력이 있어. 바로 끈적한 손바닥과 엄청 높게 점프하는 거야."
"Ron can get it easily," I said. "He can use his powers — his sticky hands and super long jumps."

론은 크게 숨을 들이마신 뒤 나무를 오르기 시작했어. 이쪽저쪽 가지 사이를 뛰어올랐지.
Ron took a deep breath and began climbing the tree, jumping from branch to branch.

론은 금세 장난감에 다가가 가지고 내려와 동생에게 건네주었어.
He reached the toy and very soon, got down and handed it to my brother.

"형은 내 영웅이야!" 대니가 활짝 웃으며 론을 힘껏 껴안았어.
"You're my hero!" Danny laughed and gave Ron a big hug.

"사실은 마야가 진짜 영웅이야." 론이 말했어. "너희 누나가 다 가르쳐 준거거든!"
"Actually, Maya is the real hero," Ron corrected him.
"She taught me everything I know! "

그날 비록 영화 속 영웅이 아니더라도, 우리는 충분히 똑똑하고, 강하고, 뭐든지 해낼 수 있다는 사실을 배웠어!
That day we learned that even if we're not the superheroes from the movies, we're smart and strong and can do anything we want!

그리고 기억해, 너희도 우리처럼 영웅이라는걸!
And remember, you are a Superhero too!